Mulligan^{2}

CAROLYN SNELLING

CREATION HOUSE
A STRANG COMPANY

Library of Congress Control Number: 2008939234
International Standard Book Number: 978-1-59979-528-7

First Edition

08 09 10 11 12 — 987654321
Printed in the United States of America

For you, O LORD, have delivered my soul from death, my eyes from tears, my feet from stumbling, that I may walk before the LORD in the land of the living.

—PSALM 116:8–9

CONTENTS

ACKNOWLEDGMENTS

T—To my parents: Thanks for your love and for funding this project! Thanks also to Bob's parents for giving birth to and nurturing such a wonderful, selfless man. Thanks as well to our family members for the joy you bring to our lives.

H—Hallelujah and all praise to God! He sent some fabulous people to help with this book: my terrific sister, Jackie Lynch; Marsha Macdonald; Michele DeFilippo and the crew at 1106 Design; and Amy Collins.

A—Awesome friends who supported me were: Carrie Fay Amaro, Mr. and Mrs. Gale Erickson, Natalie Hearn, Jessica Hovland, Theresa Jones, the Randy Rickey family, and Mona Wright.

N—Noteworthy acknowledgments: Please go to my Web site at www.heartofthecrossbooks.com to hear a song that captures my gratitude to our Lord and Savior. The Radiant Church Worship Team presents this song for you! Also, I mention the song "Come Rain or Come Shine" in the Introduction.

Thanks to Alfred Publishing Company and the Johnny Mercer Foundation for their permission to reprint a portion of the lyrics.

K—Kudos to Eva Shaw, PhD, and Tobi Taylor. Eva is a wonderful mentor! Tobi is a great editor!

S—Special thanks to my hero, my forever love, my best mulligan of all time, my hubby, Bob Snelling.

PREFACE

I THINK I MAY be part of the last generation who still likes to read the morning newspaper. I have often asked myself why I have grown so dependent on this daily ritual, particularly when most of the news seems to go from bad to worse in the blink of an eye. Sometimes I wonder if the newspaper owners tell the reporters, "OK, go out and find the worst story you can, because it will sell tomorrow's paper and you can keep your job." They really aren't reporting all of the news, but in fact are finding ways to sensationalize only the bad news. Isn't it strange that reading the paper has become this bad habit I can't shake? I guess I am an addict. Oddly enough, it brings a kind of certainty to my day. Bad things do happen. I can count on it. This certainty in my life has created a mantra for me that goes something like this: "Hope for the best, but expect the worst."

I think I can pinpoint where this cynicism comes from. No, I am not going to blame my parents. They are both deceased, and it is not my intent to use this book to fault their parenting style. They offered me the best they had to give. I would guess, in fact, that were my father here today he would say I was the boy he always wanted. He introduced me to baseball, and while I was never an athlete, with him I became a great spectator. He and I saw the Oakland Athletics play many times and were lucky enough to get tickets to a World Series game. It was a shame that I allowed boys into my life in my early teens, because I believe my desire to be in their company drove a wedge between my dad and me. However, I was with him when he was on his deathbed. He smiled at me, and with his last breath asked me to take care of my mother. In that moment, all was forgiven and forgotten. I was twenty and he was fifty-nine.

My second husband, Bob, is exactly twenty-six years my senior. OK, let's just put it right on the table. I married a father figure. I didn't have to get a master's degree in psychology to figure that one out. Did I marry him with that in mind? Of course not! I fell in love with a man who brought me unconditional love. I fell in love with the man who introduced me to Christ. Judge if you will, think what you want, for many before you have done so, as well. Odd as it may seem, it is from our beautiful relationship that my cynicism found a home.

Strange, isn't it, that something so beautiful and perfect can have a tinge of cynicism? During the early years of our budding relationship, we endured many stares and glares. We sent people through the roof when we would kiss or show any intimacy toward each other. If you suddenly are feeling like one of those cynics, it's OK. Perhaps after reading my testimony your negative opinion will be dispelled.

I was never a cynical child or teen. In fact, I was too narcissistic to be a cynic. It is true that my cynicism was born from the ridicule and heartache that my husband and I endured in those early years. Granted, our relationship was of our choosing, and thankfully, none of the ridicule or heartache ever came from our families. My mother never said a harsh word to or about Bob. My sister and her family were always accepting, and the same holds true for Bob's family.

It was ridicule by outsiders that, amazingly, hurt me the worst. You would think that if our families could accept our relationship, then why should the opinion of others matter so much? Bob has much more self-esteem than I do, and he would say, "So what?" But their disapproval hurt me at my core. At the time, I had a bachelor's degree in human relations, so you would think that so much formal education would have helped me to better understand their disgust and rise above their pettiness. But it didn't, and I couldn't. So, interestingly enough, my mantra of "Hope for the best, expect the worst" was most certainly born out of the beginnings of our beautiful relationship. I kept hoping at every turn that people, mostly women, wouldn't immediately show disfavor toward me when we were together. You don't have to have studied psychology to know that acceptance from women is important to me, and probably speaks to my relationship with my mother. Praise God she accepted Christ during the last days of her life. I miss her with every part of who I am. When I was a child and hurting, she would say, "Just smile, it only hurts for a little while."

I don't tend to show my cynical side to anyone. As far as the outside world knows, I smile and act as if I have an ability to deflect all hurt. Before I wrote this book, only God and Bob knew of my suppressed cynicism and anger. I never sought therapy, thinking that it would not be perceived well by anyone who might find out. Instead, I got a degree in psychology and then decided to write this book!

How did a positive idea such as this book come into my cynical mind? It just happened one morning as I looked up over my newspaper, which was full of bad news. I said to Bob, "Isn't it awesome how God has allowed us the privilege of living here on the golf course? Most especially how He has let us live here on the first tee?" I then thought I ought to write a book.

Living on a golf course may not be your cup of tea, but we can't imagine living anywhere else. In the midst of all the bad news this world can heap upon everyone, living here brings hope to our day. We can count on its loveliness and beauty.

We live in Surprise, Arizona, northwest of Phoenix, in a retirement community surrounded by four golf courses. The majority of people who move to this type of community would undoubtedly say that living on a golf course lot represents living life to its best and fullest. So, knowing the choices I have made in my life, many of which I cannot bring myself to share with you, why then would God allow me such a privilege? The privilege to which I am referring is living life at its best *and* having a "perfect" husband to love.

Yes, I have done many things in my life for which I am not very proud, things about which I hoped for the best and received only the worst. Maybe you can imagine them? Yes, they are that bad. My mistakes are best kept between God and myself. So, with the knowledge in my heart of all the bad things I have done, why should God have sent His only Son to die on a cross for me? Why has He favored me in so many ways, not the least of which is letting me live in a beautiful home located in such a gorgeous setting? The only answer I can imagine is because He knew I would do all those bad things and yet He loves me anyway. I am so thankful that His love is unconditional.

We Christians realize that our God is all about love. He is a totally forgiving God. Do you have any idea what a welcome relief that is for a sinner like me? Knowing this, I have often wondered why everyone in the world wouldn't embrace Christianity, for it is written in Romans 14:11, "'As surely as I live,' says the Lord, 'every knee will bow before me; every tongue will confess to God.'" We will all have to stand before Him one day, so why not be on His side now? I have heard my pastor, Lee McFarland of Radiant Church say that it is because this is the age of grace. God is giving everyone the opportunity to freely accept Him now.

How do I know He is working in my life? I know in my heart that He is with me. I wish I could be more articulate, but all I know is what my heart tells me. God has always been with me. I have unfortunately rejected Him time and time again. Before I knew Him, I thought if I tried to seek the best on my own that undoubtedly it would come. It is no wonder, then, that I found only the worst. With Him, all things are possible, but without Him, life can be very hard. In Luke 18:27, Jesus replied, "What is impossible with men is possible with God."

I was born in the 1960s and went through my formative years not understanding much about God. My parents didn't go to church and never mentioned Christ. In the 1970s, interestingly enough, I gained popularity in a religious social order—emphasis on the "social"—only to find myself memorizing scripture but living the life of an irresponsible and free-spirited youth. In the early 1980s, my life was about trying to find a career among the recreational drugs and three-martini lunches. It was finally in the 1990s that God was to deliver me from the madness of the first thirty years of my life. He sent me an incredible and unconditional love. He sent me Bob.

As I have already written, Bob is my second husband. It is very difficult for me to relate the details of my first marriage to you. But, looking back now, I don't harbor any ill will or resentment toward my first husband for our failed marriage. I must assume the lion's share of the blame for that time in our lives. I should never have married him. My marriage to him was an attempt to replace the love of my deceased father.

My first husband was extremely handsome. He looked like a Greek god: perfect in form, tall, blonde, and beautiful. Unfortunately, ours was not a match made in heaven. His interests were very different from mine. He liked water-skiing and loved everything associated with the water, including the hobby of keeping fish tanks in our home. I hated water sports and didn't care that much for the fish swimming in my living room. I liked to look at the ocean, but only from the beach while sunning myself. He was extremely analytical and appreciated the value of reason. I, on the other hand, was impulsive. Suffice it to say, his spirit and mine were about as alike as freshwater fish and saltwater fish—not a good match. I believe in my heart that he had a kind spirit. I was too self-absorbed to try to be the kind of wife who could nurture that spirit in her husband. I pray now that he enjoys that spirit with someone who will appreciate him and all of his interests. We were both very naive in our approach to marriage, and our expectations of one another at the time could never have brought forth a genuine union.

Despite an irresponsible and promiscuous youth, a failed marriage, recreational drug use, and—probably worst of all—a cynical attitude, I have still been shown great favor by God. This is why I feel I must share my testimony with you. I want to do this before I can't, before my life passes, and I say, "I wish I had told the world about God's love for me."

When I was preparing the draft of this testimony, I asked Bob to read it for me and offer his thoughts. He said, "Well, that's a great piece of fiction." I think he felt I was portraying him a bit too favorably. I then asked Dr. Eva Shaw to assist me in preparing this book for publication. If you ever write your testimony or need help with your book, call on her, for she is a great sounding board. She said, "I'm sure you think Bob is perfect, but he can't be. Remember, Carolyn, not all your readers can identify with your joy in your perfect husband."

I concede that perhaps they are both correct. However, recognizing my suppressed cynicism, it is a wonderful surprise knowing that Bob is a perfect gift from God. Meeting Bob was the one time when I hoped for the best and got it! There is no worst with him—this is how I know his love is from God. It's bizarre how life can have bad and good intertwined simultaneously. Out of my cynicism has come a beautiful and lasting relationship.

Please allow me to share with you my love for Bob using the analogy of the game of golf. Golf can have its share of ups and downs, good and bad, all in the same round. Rarely are there perfect rounds of golf. Rarely, too, are there perfect husbands. Mine may not be perfect to you, but he is my kind of perfect. I hope you will keep an open mind as you read my heart, complete the chapter activities, read the prayers, and thoughtfully consider the scripture at the end of each chapter. Each scripture reference is taken from the New International Version.

Mulligan: A Second Chance at True Love and God's Grace is my Christian testimony. It is my story of God's love at work in my life through my "perfect" husband.

INTRODUCTION

MY HUSBAND, BOB, and I live on the first tee of a beautiful golf course in Surprise, Arizona, northwest of Phoenix. Actually, our home is about one hundred yards from the men's tees. The blue or championship tees are about as far away, and the ladies' tees are only a stone's throw from our chaise lounge. You don't have to be a golf enthusiast to appreciate the beauty of this scenic locale. The first fairway sits to the right of our home. There are nine palm trees that sway in the background behind the tees. The trees seem to dominate the background of this setting. I have come to the conclusion that the course designer must have planted them according to the principles of feng shui. To the left of the tees sits a pond that has been aerated to ward off mosquitoes. Finally, topping it all off, is the majesty of the morning sun rising over the entire scene. Our breakfast nook is situated so that we get a perfect view of this amazing picture that God has created just for us. It is our slice of heaven on Earth.

Perhaps living near a golf course is not what you would consider your ideal home site. Maybe you would prefer to live among the bustle of a big city? Perhaps your tastes run more toward a home site on rocky terrain. Or maybe your idea of heaven on Earth would be to live on a desert island. For us, living on a golf course is very peaceful. It brings a calm certainty to our days. Regardless of your preferred location for your home, if you enjoy the game of golf and can appreciate the similarities between it and a successful marriage, then I hope this book will be enjoyable for you to read. Also, if you are a Christian who loves to tell others about Christ at work in your life, I hope you will enjoy this book, too.

Please don't think that you have to understand the intricacies or the terms associated with the game of golf to capture the essence of this story. I will help out along the way, with what little I know. Simply stated, the game of golf has eighteen holes to be played. Each of those holes has a designated "par" of three, four, or five strokes, or golf shots. The hope is that after a golfer has played all eighteen holes, the combined total of shots from each hole will add up to seventy-two. Clubs are used to hit the ball far distances and when approaching the green, and putters are used on the green, where the hole is found.

Although I have played this game, serious golfers would consider me a "hack."* The reason I am a hack is that I don't have a lot of patience. To commit four hours to this game in one day makes me crazy. I applaud those who can devote at least four hours per day to golf and enjoy it. However, it is very calming, while reading the newspaper, to watch the many golfers begin their day's activity practically in our backyard. They wave to us from their carts as they drive on the path that will take them on their four-hour adventure.

Not only do I not have the patience for golf, I am not athletic. I look like I am swatting flies whenever I play golf. Also, I will occasionally "whiff" the ball.** It is so infuriating when that little white ball just sits there almost smiling back at me, with all its dimples, and says, "Hey dummy, you're supposed

---

* A hack is someone who plays golf once in a while and basically just "hacks" the ball around.

** This means attempting to strike the ball with the club and missing—badly.

to hit me." Or better still, when I do make contact with the ball, it has actually been known to go backwards. I don't know how I do it. It can be very funny to watch. The first time I hit it backwards, Bob said, "Whoa, that's a first." If backwards golf ever becomes a sport, I will sign up for it.

My poor eyesight has been a hindrance to successful hand-eye coordination, which is a must in most sports. Bob, on the other hand, has great hand-eye coordination. He was quite a golfer in his early days of playing, and I will write more about that later. It was he who introduced me to the game. Although he loves the sport and has devoted the majority of his life to it, interestingly enough, I wouldn't say that the game has made him a patient person.

He and I are very similar in so many ways, not the least of which is that we are both control freaks. You might think that this would be cause for consternation in our household, but that has not been the case. We lose patience with people we don't know, like rude drivers. Neither of us likes to stand in long lines. We also lose patience with our dog, though her behavior is clearly our fault and not hers. Bob can lose patience while playing golf, but, generally speaking, he is able to keep his frustration to himself. We rarely, if ever, lose patience with each other.

Although I am a hack, I have played enough rounds to realize that when a golfer steps up to the first tee, this usually means he is full of hope, joy, and freedom. I think these aspects represent, to a tee, the elements of our marriage.

I am now fourteen years into my second marriage, and it is a very happy one. My first marriage was not. I approached it much like a hack, not taking it seriously. The majority of our days were filled with nothing but hurt and sorrow and a great deal of impatience with each other. Given that I approached my first marriage like a hack, why, then, would God show favor on me and give me a second chance at marriage? *Well, in golf, there's a term for a second chance—a mulligan—in which a golfer has the opportunity to retake an errant shot. Bob, you see, is my mulligan from God.*

This book is my Christian testimony; it is my way of saying thanks to God for giving me a second chance for a happy marriage. Now that I have received Christ as my Lord and Savior, I pray for my first husband and honestly wish him well.

I never want to repeat the same mistakes with my second husband. I always want him to know how precious he is to me. Thanks to God, I find myself now living every day of my marriage "on the first tee," literally and figuratively, for when a golfer steps up to the first tee, this usually means that he or she is full of hope. Stepping up to the first tee can bring on a sense of great joy and freedom, as my second marriage has done.

This book contains what I believe are three keys to a happy marriage. The keys will be represented by three chapters: the first on listening, the second on respect, and the third on love. Each chapter has one or two activities and prayer for your consideration, as well as some scripture related to each chapter's topic. Hearing God's word on each topic helps bring things into focus for me. I hope it will do that for you, too. I considered writing a fourth chapter on humor, but then my bad memory got the better of me.

I said to Bob as I was writing, "Quick, say something funny so that I can write it down." He replied, "You're a nut." I said, "I know, but seriously, name some funny things that have happened or that we have said that were funny." Giving his typical Bob

Snelling answer, he said, "First of all, what is funny to us may not be funny to the readers. Second, if you can't remember, then it must not have been that funny."

I do recall one funny thing that happened between us early on in our relationship. To better understand this story, you need to know that Bob and I love all kinds of music, and one of our favorite singers is Frank Sinatra. We were dining in a romantic restaurant in south San Francisco late one Saturday afternoon, when Bob started humming a tune.

I remarked, "That's nice, where did you hear that?"

He replied, "Oh, it's just a little song that I have been working on for you."

"You wrote me a song?"

Without uttering an answer, he looked at me with his beautiful hazel eyes and started to sing, "I'm gonna love you, like nobody's loved you, come rain or come shine, happy together and unhappy together and won't it be fine. Days may be cloudy or sunny, we're in or we're out of the money. I'll love you baby, come rain or come shine."

My heart was racing so fast at the thought of

him writing a song for me—and one that sounded so good, too. I went on for several months thinking how wonderful it was that he would write a song just for me. Well, lo and behold, I was in the car alone one day, and I heard Frank Sinatra on my radio singing *my* song. When I saw Bob later in the day, I said, "Oh by the way, thanks so much for that great song. When did you sell it to Sinatra?"

He laughed a little devilish laugh like that of a young boy who knows he was just caught with his hand in the cookie jar. It was harmless fun and to this day is cause for a lot of laughter, particularly when we tell our friends who remember the song. I wonder if they think, "Oh, that Bob," or "Gee whiz, is she that gullible?" Maybe Bob is right and that isn't funny to you, but it was to us. I guess we all have our own kind of humor. The point is laughter is an important element of a successful marriage.

We laugh with each other every day and poke fun at one another. Lord knows that Bob has *a lot* of material in me. I mentioned that I have zero hand-eye coordination, but I don't think that has much to do with the fact that I am a klutz. Bob has often said that I can break something just by looking at it.

However, I will say that as klutzy as I certainly

know I can be, my beautiful and perfect husband is clearly what I would have to characterize as "handyman-challenged." Wouldn't you think that if I break it, he should fix it? But that's not how it is in our household. Have you ever heard the joke about how many people it takes to fix something? In our house, it takes both of us and then probably a few more people to get the job done.

Not long ago, we needed to replace a light bulb in one of our ceiling fan light kits. Granted, this was not a bulb that was easily reached. It happened to involve a fourteen-foot ceiling and a light kit whose domed face needed to come off before the bulb could be replaced. Bob, in his impatience, took a screwdriver to the dome face of the light kit. Needless to say, the dome would not readily pop away from its housing. I was holding the ladder during this process, making certain that I didn't utter a word. After the dome cracked, I still didn't make a peep. I knew that he realized what he had done was incredibly misguided. It took everything I had to be silent. Eventually, we were able to replace the bulb. Notice the emphasis on "we."

I have to share one final funny incident, and I do this with Bob's blessing. We own a rental property here in Arizona. The smoke alarm at this property kept beeping, beeping, beeping. Every time we went to the property, Bob would diligently climb a step-stool to try to reset the alarm. He even replaced the battery in the alarm, believing that surely that must be the problem. He finally bought a new smoke alarm, which didn't solve the problem; this beeping went on for many months. We didn't have a renter in the property, so we just let it be. Finally, when we had a renter arriving soon, Bob decided that he would call in a handyman. The handyman came over and asked Bob if he had changed the batteries in *all* the alarms. Bob asked, "What all, aren't there only two?" The handyman replied, "No, there are at least four. You have one in each bedroom, one in the hallway, and one in the kitchen. If all the batteries aren't fresh, it will affect the one." Bob looked stunned. "Oh, really? What a ditz!" he exclaimed.

My ability to break everything and his inability to fix things has made for a lot of laughter in our house. Actually, the laughter comes after things have finally been fixed, but it still comes.

Golf, too, can be a sport in which many laughs are found. Most of the laughter comes later, at the nineteenth hole. For my non-golfing friends, the nineteenth hole is where refreshment and laughter can be found. Serious golfers are prone to certain emotions while they play a round of golf, and usually that doesn't involve laughter. It is amazing to watch the transformation that takes place: a person starts off a round of golf with a smile and a handshake, and by the end of eighteen holes he or she is an uptight, impatient mess. Needless to say, the nineteenth hole is a place to unwind and regain some joy from what can sometimes be a harrowing event. On the other hand, if a golfer has shot "par" or better,* then he or she will enjoy many laughs at the nineteenth hole.

While golf and the Snelling marriage have been filled with laughter, I give thanks to God that He has a sense of humor too! You know immediately the things that make you laugh, and we have God to thank for all of it. I will pray for a lot of laughter in your marriage and in your life!

---

* Shooting par or better means that the golfer played eighteen holes with the prescribed number of strokes or fewer.

chapter 1

FORE! THE JOY OF LISTENING

WHEN I SHARED with Bob that I was writing this book, he gave me the following as an opening line: "As I strode to the first tee, I found myself happy and excited about the great day ahead of me. I have the same feelings about my husband, though they are much stronger now than the day we were married." He's funny, but he's right. I am happier and more excited after fourteen years of marriage than I was on the day we exchanged vows. I wake up each morning thanking God for him. Bob makes my heart leap and makes me thankful to be alive.

What keeps our "game" of marriage under par? (Remember, non-golfers, that's a good thing.) The first key to our successful marriage is the joy of listening. For those of you who play golf, you know that if you've hit the ball and it has the potential of interfering with the group ahead, then you should shout, *"Fore!"* You are forewarning the group in front of you that trouble is headed their way, and they should pay attention. When I hear that word on the golf course, I duck for cover. Now you can see how important listening is in the game of golf. It's the same in marriage.

Bob is clearly a better listener than I am, and of course a better golfer, too. (He has played the game for more than sixty years. He was an all-American at Stanford University in the 1950s.) Even though he's a better listener than I am, I truly love to listen to the sound of his voice. Bob could say anything, and it would be like music to my ears. I know that sounds corny, but it's true. I would rather listen to the sound of his voice than any other sound there is to hear. He never speaks without having given a good deal of thought to what he will say. He is thoughtful about how he says things, rather than just blurting out something hurtful or offensive.

We recently went shopping, because I needed a new pair of jeans. Bob loves to shop and is my best critic. I was unhappy that the size I tried on was not fitting as I would have liked. Usually I come out of the dressing room to show him the fit, but that day, I just came out ready to leave the store. He didn't say anything at the time. After we got home he told me, "Don't feel bad, honey; you are still wearing the same size in your closet. Remember, you are eight pounds less than you were last year, and different manufacturers cut the clothes differently." In that moment, I felt much better. He had listened to me at the store, he'd come up with the best response for me, and he'd waited for the right time to say it.

Sometimes I don't want to talk about something when it's occurring. For me, it is better to leave it alone until I bring it up again. After fourteen years of marriage, Bob recognizes this as one of my many fundamental weaknesses and has learned how I will best receive his help.

As I said, I love to listen to his voice, especially when he is talking about business, when we talk about God, or when he is telling me about a book he is reading. One reason I enjoy listening to him talk about business is that it reminds me of how we met. During the late 1980s, when I was in my late 20s, I was in the management-training program of a small community bank in California, and Bob was the chief operating officer. When I first joined the bank Bob couldn't understand why I was being hired. We had met a year or so prior to my joining the bank, at a Christmas party that was being hosted by my previous employer. I was asked to join the bank by the chairman of the board; although Bob had responsibility for the new management trainees, the chairman did not inform him that he had hired me. Bob was not thrilled about my joining the bank, because at that time hiring management from the "outside" was not in keeping with its corporate culture.

Once I was hired, I had the good fortune of sitting in on many meetings at which Bob spoke, and I saw that he had everyone's attention. They all respected what he had to say about taking care of our employees, who would then take care of our customers. His coworkers believed him, because they knew that what he was saying was true. They realized that when he spoke, whatever he was saying would come to pass. Bob talked about his love for the bank and the people—employees and customers alike—and he had the influence to carry out his ideas. This bank was Bob's sole employer for fifty-four years; forty-one as an employee and fifteen as an employee and board member. After he retired as an employee, he continued to serve for thirteen more years as a board member. This kind of tenure is unheard of today, where five years with one company is practically an eternity.

Although Bob retired from the board in 2007, employees (both retired and current), board members, and customers still send him birthday cards and call him for business advice. One retired employee recently called to tell him of her health predicament, as she didn't want Bob to hear about it from another source. I don't know of another man in a work situation who has ever been more revered than he.

At the time I joined the bank, Bob was married to a woman named Mary, who has been described to me by others as a saint. Mary died in 1990 from bone cancer. Mary and Bob were married right out of high school. They had one daughter, Teri, and I am proud to call her both family and friend. I'll talk more about Teri and the rest of our family in the last chapter of this book.

After Mary passed away, Bob and I began to spend a good deal of time together at company functions, golf outings, auctions, and a variety of community fundraisers, because publicly representing the bank was a big part of our respective jobs. During those times, we found out how much we enjoyed being together and how much we had in common.

For example, we both *love* all types of sports, especially baseball. We watch baseball on television and go to professional games in downtown Phoenix when we can. We like to attend the spring training games here in Arizona each March. We count ourselves particularly blessed to have a spring training ballpark here in Surprise. So, we are able to watch baseball March through October, as fall league ball is big around here, too. We also share the same political views. We love to read, although Bob likes contemporary fiction, while I prefer classic novels and history. We love Hawaii—in fact, we love it so much, we were married there. We love to talk with each other, and are each other's best friend. We love to be alone, and more than anything, we found out that we laugh and cry at the same things. Bob is wonderful about going to "chick flicks." Sometimes, as we are watching the movie, I will hear him sniffling more than I do.

You can imagine the naysayers who tried to throw cold water on our relationship, criticizing us for our age difference. He is, as I already mentioned, twenty-six years my senior. Yes, there were those, especially women, who were at the time very hurtful. They would make comments like, "Oh, she's just a gold digger," or "He's old enough to be her father—how could they?" Worse still were the glares of disgust we would get from, yes, mostly women. But despite those hurtful moments, we knew what we had was so special that we would happily endure any criticism. As I age, the glares are less frequent. Now I am wondering if I don't yearn for those glares. However, not long ago, as I went to introduce Bob to an acquaintance of mine, this person said, "Oh, is this your dad?" Bob and I just laughed.

To this day, we take time to listen to each other's hearts. When our friendship began, Bob's heart, of course, was still in mourning for Mary. They, too, had a lifelong friendship. I often times feel guilty that I am now enjoying the fruits of what they built for so many years. Bob has often said, "I was never the husband that she deserved." Well, that is just silly, for as wonderful as I am sure she was, he is a man among men, the best, the greatest. They must have brought a joy beyond words to those whose lives they, as a couple, touched.

The most important thing I know about Mary is that she planted the seed of Christ in Bob's heart. Bob recently accepted Jesus as his Lord and Savior, and was baptized on June 10, 2006. I have been a Christian since 1995. I love to listen to Bob's perspective on God. He is so humble when he talks about the most humble Human who ever lived.

For many years, Bob did not attend church regularly. However, when we lived in California, the minister who performed Mary's funeral watered the seed she had planted in Bob's heart. The minister's name is Larry Vilardo. He is a very easygoing, down-to-earth guy who is always ready with a smile and word of encouragement, much like Bob. The church he serves, Rockville Presbyterian, is small, with perhaps about two hundred members. Although Bob loves Pastor Larry, he wasn't ready to commit himself to Christ at that time.

After we married, I told Bob I wanted to thank God for sending me such an amazing and selfless husband; the unconditional love I feel from Bob could come only from the Most High. So, Bob sent me to Rockville, and I loved it there. I would come home after service, and we would talk about God. I asked Bob questions about something God wrote in the Word, or something that His Son Jesus had said. Bob would always give me an answer that was full of love, understanding, and hope. When he didn't understand something, he would admit it and encourage me not to question God. Bob would say, "His ways are greater than ours, honey," and, "We just have to trust in Him." I think Bob's life verse should be Proverbs 3:5–6, "Trust in the LORD with all your heart and lean not on your own understanding; in all your ways acknowledge him, and he will make your paths straight." Do you see why I had to write this love story?

Bob totally understands God. His faith is stronger than mine will ever be. Even though he is a baby Christian, he has known Christ all his life. He understands Him without fully understanding. He believes without seeing. He trusts not knowing what lies ahead in this world. He lives and loves as Christ has asked us. I pray that your spouse provides this for you. Maybe, like Bob before he officially accepted Christ, your spouse doesn't attend church even though you wish he or she would? I prayed for the longest time that Bob would accept Christ and that he would start going to church. God answered my prayer in May 2005.

We moved to Arizona in August 2001. It took me a while to find a church home here. However, I finally settled on a small church much like the one I attended in California. In order to grow the congregation of this church, I was asked to go on a "recon" mission. I wanted to discover how some of the larger churches attract and retain members. There is one mega-church near us called Radiant Church, where dressing in casual clothing is encouraged. In fact, this church is known as "the blue jean" church. Knowing that Bob loves to wear his shorts year-round—one of the reasons we relocated to Arizona—I said, "Hey, would you like to come with me to church on Sunday, and you can wear your shorts?" He exclaimed, "What, are you kidding?" I explained to him the atmosphere he could expect: casual dressers, rock-and-roll worship music, and, best yet, no one would know him. He wouldn't have to socialize if he didn't want to. This last point was especially attractive to Bob, as he will tell you he is a hermit at heart. It used to bother him when he would go to smaller churches and someone would say, "We missed you last week," as if they were tracking his attendance. I am sure these people were just trying to be friendly, but to

Bob it was a turnoff. I must admit that sometimes his isolationist mentality has made for a few challenges, as I tend to be gregarious and am in need of Christian fellowship. Bob would truly be happy on a desert island.

Everything about Radiant Church sounded good to Bob, so off we went. Between Pastor Lee McFarland's humorous and relevant Bible-based teachings, the exceptional rock-and-roll music, the coffee shop, and free doughnuts, Bob was hooked. These methods of recruitment may not sit well with some traditionalists, but they have brought us closer to God. Bob has had more desire to learn about God and His Word in these last few years than ever before. If it takes humor and a cup of fancy coffee to help him feel relaxed and inspired to know God, then why not? Some may feel as if this kind of atmosphere is not respectful, but nothing could be further from the truth. There is a greater sense of respect and worship for our Creator in the Snelling house now than there was in the previous years of our marriage. We read Scripture together each day from the *One Year Bible,* which is set up like a daily devotional. Each day we read passages from the Old Testament and New Testament, a psalm, and a proverb. It takes only about ten minutes. Don't we all have a few minutes for God, especially a few minutes as husband and wife and God? In addition, each of us reads on alternate days. Afterward, we talk about what we've read, and then we move on with the day. It is an inexpressible joy for me to know that Bob is now saved!

I was so happy with Radiant Church that I began to volunteer in its bookstore. Shortly afterward, a position came open on the staff as the human resources manager. I could never have predicted that working in the bank's human resources department and in public relations would prove valuable in church ministry. Thanks to God, I was selected to serve. Anyone who works in church ministry recognizes what an honor it is to work on holy ground.

Working at Radiant Church was one of the greatest experiences I will ever know. Unfortunately, the time demands that are required in ministry left Bob and me little time to enjoy his golden years. I struggled mightily with my decision to leave the staff. On the one hand, I wanted to work for God in His church, giving up for Him the one thing that meant the most to me—my time with Bob. On the other hand, Bob and I missed each other very much and felt as if our precious time together was passing us by. Apparently, I am still not yet willing to lay it all down for God. I do believe, however, that my decision to leave was in the best interest of our marriage. We are, however, both still active members. I volunteer there, and Bob has accepted a spot on Radiant's advisory board. When Bob first accepted Christ, he struggled to identify his ministry. He found that his leadership and financial expertise fit the needs of this ministry perfectly—to a "tee." The meetings are held once a month, so the demand on his time is not great. Isn't it awesome how God brings us all around for His good purposes.

We give thanks to Bob's first wife, Mary, Pastor Larry Vilardo, and Pastor Lee McFarland, as well as our friends at Rockville and Radiant churches for touching Bob's life in order to bring him to Christ. Most especially, we give thanks to God! To Him is all the glory!

When we aren't reading Scripture together, I also love to listen to Bob when he is telling me the plot of whatever book he is reading. I already mentioned that Bob loves to read contemporary fiction. He reads about the daring ladies' man, who, in about one minute, will save the world from certain destruction. I, on the other hand, like to read poetry or classics like the novels of Jane Austen, Dostoevsky, and Tolstoy, so contemporary fiction is not really my cup of tea. But when Bob recounts a tale, I am on the edge of my seat. He can tell a story better than the writer. I can't wait for him to keep reading so he can tell me the rest of the tale. He injects all of the necessary inflections into the story. I think it is just his voice, with its soft, easy, and calming cadence. He has a gleam in his hazel eyes when he is about to recount how the hero has cleverly and single-handedly thwarted and outsmarted the most devious terrorist or criminal mastermind.

Bob also has that gleam in his eye when he is engaged in conversation with business associates and friends. Bob has a few close friends who are truly great blessings in his life. He enjoys each of them and might just be tempted to ask them to join him on that desert island.

When Bob talks, people listen. As I said, I'd prefer to listen to his voice over any other sound on the planet. The only greater sound I can imagine, however, is the sound of trumpets announcing Jesus' second coming!

When I began to decide how I wanted to present this book to you, I honestly wanted you to hear my heart. I wanted to tell you how thankful I am to God for all He has done. I also wanted to share with you some things that I do or have done that serve as daily reminders for me about how blessed I feel. Also, there are prayers that I pray and scripture that I love, which I hope you will enjoy, too. Perhaps you will use them to supplement your own favorites. Regardless, I hope that the activities, prayers, and scripture will be useful to you.

As we have now reached the end of the first chapter, I truly, sincerely, most earnestly, want to encourage you to enjoy listening to your spouse. Maybe you are already great at listening to him or her, and if that listening brings you joy, then I am thrilled for you. But if you are challenged in this area, I can only offer you something that someone once told me: "There must be a reason God gave us two ears and just one mouth." I have to keep reminding myself of this every day, not just with

Bob, but with everyone. I have learned so much from Bob. One of the best things he has taught me, without having to tell me, is to try to be a better listener.

Chapter Activity

Think of a situation or situations where you enjoy listening to your spouse. Is it when he or she is speaking to you, your children, or your grand-children? Is it when you hear him or her with friends or strangers? When your spouse talks with you, what does he or she say that just "rocks your world"? If you journal, it might be good to keep these things written on a special page that you can refer to on a regular basis. Think about these good things, and try not to dwell on the times when your spouse doesn't listen to you as you might wish. The more you dwell on what's wrong, the less you will hold onto what's right.

Prayer Time

Are you the best listener you can be for your spouse? If yes, I hope you will give thanks to God for this blessing and what must certainly be a great marriage. If not, maybe ask God what you can do to improve your desire to be a better listener. Try to find the joy in listening. Try not to focus, as I tend to do, on what you want or what you need to say—just listen. You never know when you will no longer have the opportunity to listen to him or her.

God knows that among my greatest fears is realizing the day will come when I will no longer hear Bob's voice. As a Christian, you would think I would recognize the importance of our being called home to be with the Lord and be happy about it. For me, though, if Bob is called first, the thought of not being able to hear his voice will bring about an unbearable sadness and silence. So I pray:

> *Dear God, thank You so very much for every word that comes from Bob's mouth and every day that You allow me to hear it. You are an awesome God to show me such favor with a husband who listens and loves as he does. I love You, God. Help me to be the best wife for him, one who always listens with great care and who always lets him know how precious he is to me and to everyone he touches. Thank You for allowing me the privilege of listening to him. I thank You in the*

*name of Your Son Jesus Christ, our Lord
and Savior. Amen.*

He who answers before listening—that is his
folly and his shame.

—PROVERBS 18:13

Listen to advice and accept instruction, and in
the end you will be wise.

—PROVERBS 19:20

Ears that hear and eyes that see—the LORD has
made them both.

—PROVERBS 20:12

Blessed is the man who listens to me, watching
daily at my doors, waiting at my doorway. For
whoever finds me finds life and receives favor
from the LORD. But whoever fails to find me
harms himself; all who hate me love death.

—PROVERBS 8:34–36

chapter 2

THANK YOU FOR THE GAME:
THE IMPORTANCE OF RESPECT

GOLF HAS BEEN called a gentlemen's sport. In fact, someone once told me that *golf* stands for "gentlemen only, ladies forbidden." Many lady golfers out there would vehemently deny this acronym! Regardless, golf is about acting as a gentleman or a lady should; it's about acting respectfully while you play. It's about taking your turn when you are supposed to, and shaking hands with your playing partners at the beginning and end of the round. It's about fixing your divots and tending to your pitch marks.*

---

* Divots are chunks of grass (either on the fairway or in the rough) that have been displaced after a golfer has taken his or her swing. When a golfer reaches the green and finds that his or her approach shot has made an indentation, that is called a pitch mark. In both cases, it is a courtesy to replace the chunk of grass and tend to the pitch mark.

31

Additionally, the respect associated with golf means not moving or making a sound when another golfer is about to strike the ball with the club or putter. It's about not walking in someone else's line—the space between the golfer's ball and the hole. It's about not expectorating on the golf course. It's about helping another golfer find his or her ball if it has strayed off the fairway. It's most especially about playing with integrity.

For example, if a golfer commits a penalty while the others with whom he or she is playing have gone to play their respective shots, then the golfer needs to bring that penalty to the attention of the other players. This will result in one or more strokes being added to his or her score. Unlike in other sports, a higher score (more strokes) is *not* the desired result in golf.

In all of the years that I have known Bob, I can count on him to show me respect through his integrity. Move over George Washington, Bob has *never* told a lie (God is my witness). We have been in a variety of situations, with a variety of people. He tells the truth *always*. It may not be what the person wants to hear, but he tempers it in such a way that it comes across as gentle and caring.

When I asked Bob to tell me what he considers the most important courtesies one golfer can show to another, he said, "Be respectful; be honest."

In our marriage, Bob *always* shows me respect. The second key to our successful marriage has been the importance of respect. Bob never hurts my feelings. He treats me like a precious treasure. His courtesy toward me is best characterized by the word *gentleman*. He never, for one minute or one interaction, takes our familiarity for granted. If we are socializing with another couple, he would never correct something I said in front of them. He has never scolded me or even offered me a gentle correction. I think it's because he is hoping I will come to the realization on my own that I made a mistake and said something I shouldn't have.

His gentle demeanor also explains why he is such a great parent to Teri. He has told me that when Teri was a child he would provide the necessary correction, but he recalls her being a "good girl," so she didn't need much in the way of discipline. She, in turn, is an incredible parent. I have always marveled at her parenting skills. I will never forget an interaction she had with our grandson Cameron when he was a toddler. Teri was busy cooking dinner while she was chatting on the phone. Cameron came to her, as most toddlers will, and was looking for her complete attention. In a very gentle manner, she stopped cooking, got off the phone, and gave Cameron her undivided attention. From that point on, I became her fan. I believe that parenting skills are taught to children. When children become parents, they mirror how they were treated. Congratulations to Bob and Mary for the excellent job they have done with Teri. They have certainly inspired responsible parents for generations to come.

Bob, although he has good reason to be, is *never* boastful. He has such a quiet spirit; it's not timid nor should it be seen as a weakness. In fact, his humility and quiet nature are great strengths. I believe that this is why he is revered by so many. I can see God's grace shining through him each day, in every way, through the things he says and how he acts toward me and others.

When I was putting my ideas together for this chapter, I came up with a list of things Bob would *never* do and a list of things that he *always* does to show me respect.

Never

- Uses a cell phone in public
- Finishes another person's sentence
- Walks ahead of me
- Blows his nose in public
- Coughs without covering his mouth and saying, "Excuse me"
- Insults me
- Hurts me
- Uses profanity
- Says he will do something and then doesn't follow through
- Cuts in line
- Takes our Lord's name in vain

Always

- Removes his cap at sporting events during the singing of the National Anthem
- Removes his cap in restaurants
- Opens all doors for me
- Pulls out chairs for me
- Says "thank you" and "excuse me" to everyone, including me
- Greets me with a smile and a kiss
- Lets me know that he loves me

- Is honest
- Understands that God's ways are better than our own

The best way I can share with you how Bob respects me is to say that he lets me be me. He doesn't try to change me or alter the decisions I make. I have had a lot of harebrained ideas during our marriage, and he has indulged me in every one of them.

After Bob retired in 1994 from the bank, I continued to work for another three years. However, I got tired of the commute and missed spending time with him, so I left the bank in 1997. I soon decided that I wasn't ready to play golf full-time and live the retired life, though Bob certainly deserved it. I, on the other hand, had worked for only seventeen years and didn't feel comfortable claiming the title of "retired." Instead, I decided to become an independent sales representative for a cosmetics company.

Bob helped me install software on our computer that would allow me to track my customers, their invoices, and my inventory; I would have been lost without his help. Unfortunately, my business was a complete flop. I had too much inventory on hand of items that I didn't need and didn't sell. I didn't last long in that business. When we moved to Arizona, it was a relief to not bring the business with me. Instead of saying, "I failed," I used the excuse of our move and taking care of Bob's mom as a reason not to make a success of the business. Bob never said anything about it or criticized my efforts; he quietly let me sell off my inventory for a lot less than what I paid for it.

During that time, I decided to go back to school to get my master's degree. The only thing Bob said was, "What are your plans, once you have it?" I told him that I didn't have a clue. He never said anything, but let me go ahead. Fortunately, as I already mentioned, my formal education proved useful when I worked in the church ministry as the human resources manager. Bob drove me to school most nights, because I'm not a good night driver. He would patiently read a novel in the school library while I was in class. This went on for two years. As I reached the end and was working on my thesis, I wrote thirteen drafts until my advisory committee was satisfied. Can you imagine the hair-pulling, late-night sessions that went on in the

Snelling household? As a result, Bob is today what I would call "follically challenged."

Now, several years later, I have decided to once again sell a company's products, though this company is not limited to just cosmetics. Praise God I do not have to hold any inventory on hand, either. Additionally, I have been accepted to a local university to pursue a doctoral degree. It seems like déjà vu, but I hope I have learned from my previous experiences. Bob's only comment about my new business venture was, "Maybe we should look on this as a ministry; what do you think?" About school, he said, "Do you have to do a thesis?" I replied, "Thinking of the business as a ministry sounds right," and told him, "No thesis, but I have to do a dissertation and residency." We may both be completely bald by the time I finish school. I told him there was good news this time, as my classes are online. I think he was relieved that he wasn't going to have to drive me anywhere; if you have ever driven in downtown Phoenix at rush hour, you know that it is a nightmare. Bob has set up my new business and has helped me reconfigure a workspace in our home to accommodate both my business and schooling needs.

He and our dog, Pookie (she is a cross between a Poodle and a Yorkie, hence the name), help me deliver catalogs for my business. It is a fun family event.

As you see, Bob lets me be me. Fortunately, all my harebrained schemes have not cost him much money. My mother was generous in paying for my master's coursework. I was very happy that she was able to see me graduate, all thanks to her and my father. Now several years later, I can once again thank them both for leaving me a small inheritance out of which I can pay for my doctoral studies, support my independent sales business, and self-publish this testimony.

Bob clearly respects my individuality, and I pray to God that I do that for him. Bob expresses his individuality through golf. It is a competitive sport, and he loves that aspect of the game. However, what attracts him is not competing against others, it's competing against himself. Can he beat his previous score? He acknowledges that his level of play is not what it was in his youth, but his desire to play his best is still strong.

Admittedly, however, it is somewhat distressing to me when he comes home after a round of golf and I ask him how it went. He'll say, "Lousy." When I ask him how poorly he did, he'll say, "Oh I shot seventy-nine." Seventy-nine? For the benefit of my non-golfing readers, on most golf courses, seventy-two is generally considered par. I usually shoot one-hundred and twenty! How can he complain about having to take seventy-nine? Seriously, though, if I communicate nothing else to you, please know that I respect my husband for who he is, all that he does, and for who God has made him to be.

He carries with him at all times a respect and reverence for God. In turn, God has given Bob an incredible amount of grace. If you look up *grace* in the dictionary, it has a multitude of definitions. When describing grace as it pertains to Bob, I would choose: "charm," "ease" (toward me especially), and "kindness." Perhaps the most apt description is "the influence or spirit of God operating in man to regenerate him or strengthen him."

Speaking of God, Bob, and grace, I am reminded of an acronym for the word *grace* that was used by a friend of mine from Rockville Presbyterian. Her name was Pat Bennett, and she has since passed into our Lord's care.

G — God's
R — Riches
A — At
C — Christ's
E — Expense

Pat was a very strong Christian. I remember her telling our small Bible study group that when people claimed she used her religion as a crutch, she would say, "You bet." Pat understood how we are all richly blessed because of what Christ did for us. He gave His life so that all of us could have life. I am constantly in awe of that thought, aren't you? The thought that He would die so that I might know life is nothing short of unfathomable.

Grace, respect, and reverence are common themes throughout the Bible. I notice these themes most especially when I read the Old Testament. God continually showed grace to all of our ancestors, despite their rebellion and their sin. It makes me sad each time I read a passage from the Old Testament about their rebellion. Time and time again, they refused to accept or obey Him.

You know what, though? I have accepted Him, but I still rebel. I am still too focused on myself. Who am I to criticize others when they don't accept Him, and they sin? I keep forgetting that only God can judge, and only He knows a person's heart.

Bob never forgets that. He never judges others with a critical or unforgiving heart. He always shows respect for God in honoring and being honest with others. Thanks to God for my husband, a man of honor, a man filled with respect for himself, his family, his friends, his former coworkers, me, and especially God.

Chapter Activity

Memorize this life verse:

> However, each one of you also must love his wife as he loves himself, and the wife must respect her husband.
>
> —EPHESIANS 5:33

Ask yourself these questions; you may be surprised at your answers.

- Ladies: Do you give your husband his space, or are you constantly bothering him about this or that? I am a terrible nag. I can't believe Bob puts up with it. Why should he? If I need to change him, why did I marry him? Why can't I just let him be? Do you finish his sentences for him? (This is a hard one for me. Why do I feel the need to rob him of his thoughts?)

- Gentlemen: Do you honor your wife in front of others? Bob would never share my weaknesses with others, not even in a joking way.

- Ladies and gentlemen: Do you honor each other in the small things? Have you ever been preparing the table for dinner and a napkin falls on the floor? Do you then give it to your spouse or keep it for yourself? That seems like a little thing, but God sees everything, and God is in the details.

Again, list the ways in which you respect your spouse in your journal. In this way, a gentleman can be reminded at all times and in all ways to show his wife the love she craves, and a lady can do the same for the respect and honor that her husband most certainly desires.

Prayer Time

Do you feel that you can't show respect to your spouse? Why not? If you can't do any or one of the above activities, then you may want to pray to God for help in your marriage and perhaps seek counseling. If you can show respect and love and are happy in these things, then don't forget to thank God during your prayer time for His grace that is displayed in you. If you are like me, hoping to show more grace in all situations, let's pray that God will show both of us many more ways to respect and love our spouse.

> *Dear God, thank You for the grace You show me and my husband each day. I have not shown You or my husband in all ways and all things the grace that you both deserve, yet time and time again You have shown it to me. Most especially, You showed me by sending Your Son to die for me. Help me, God, to be a better wife in Your sight. Help me know grace. I don't want to be harsh, cynical, judgmental, or rebellious. I know that I am in so many ways, so I pray that You will help me in*

this. I pray it in the name of Your Son Jesus Christ, our Lord and Savior. Amen.

In case you are wondering about the word *fear* as it appears in the scripture below, my pastor says the word should be translated as "respect."

> Charm is deceptive and beauty is fleeting, but a woman who fears the LORD is to be praised.
> —PROVERBS 31:30

> Fear the LORD, you his saints, for those who fear him lack nothing. The lions may grow weak and hungry, but those who seek the LORD lack no good thing. Come my children, listen to me, I will teach you the fear of the LORD. Whoever of you loves life and desires to see many good days, keep your tongue from evil and your lips from speaking lies. Turn from evil and do good; seek peace and pursue it. The eyes of the LORD are on the righteous and his ears are attentive to their cry.
> —PSALM 34:9–15

> These commandments that I give you today are to be upon your hearts. Impress them on your children. Talk about them when you sit at home and when you walk along the road,

when you lie down and when you get up. Tie them as symbols on your hands and bind them on your foreheads. Write them on the doorframes of your houses and on your gates. When the LORD your God brings you into the land he swore to your fathers, to Abraham, Isaac and Jacob to give you—a land with large, flourishing cities you did not build, houses filled with all kinds of good things you did not provide, wells you did not dig, and vineyards and olive groves you did not plant—then when you eat and are satisfied be careful that you do not forget the LORD, who brought you out of Egypt, out of the land of slavery. Fear the LORD your God, serve him only and take your oaths in his name. Do not follow other gods, the gods of the peoples around you, for the LORD your God, who is among you, is a jealous God and his anger will burn against you, and he will destroy you from the face of the land. Do not test the LORD your God as you did at Massah. Be sure to keep the commands of the LORD your God and the stipulations and decrees he has given you. Do what is right and good in the LORD's sight, so that it may go well with you and you may go in and take over the good land that the LORD promised on oath to your forefathers, thrusting out all your enemies before you, as the LORD said.

—DEUTERONOMY 6:6–19

As for you, you were dead in your transgressions and sins, in which you used to live when you followed the ways of this world and of the ruler of the kingdom of the air, the spirit who is now at work in those who are disobedient. All of us also lived among them at one time, gratifying the cravings of our sinful nature and following its desires and thoughts. Like the rest, we were by nature objects of wrath. But because of his great love for us, God, who is rich in mercy, made us alive with Christ even when we were dead in transgressions—it is by grace you have been saved. And God raised us up with Christ and seated us with him in the heavenly realms in Christ Jesus in order that in the coming ages He might show the incomparable riches of his grace, expressed in his kindness to us in Christ Jesus. For it is by grace you have been saved, through faith—and this not from yourselves, it is the gift of God—not by works, so that no one can boast. For we are God's workmanship, created in Christ Jesus to do

good works, which God prepared in advance
for us to do.

—EPHESIANS 2:1–10

Therefore, since we have been justified through
faith, we have peace with God through our
Lord Jesus Christ, through whom we have
gained access by faith into this grace in which
we now stand. And we rejoice in the hope of
the glory of God. Not only so, but we also
rejoice in our sufferings, because we know
that suffering produces perseverance; perseverance; character and character, hope. And
hope does not disappoint us, because God has
poured out His love into our hearts by the
Holy Spirit, whom He has given us. You see, at
just the right time, when we were still power-
less, Christ died for the ungodly. Very rarely
will anyone die for a righteous man, though
for a good man someone might possibly dare
to die. But God demonstrates his own love for
us is this: While we were still sinners, Christ
died for us. Since we have now been justified
by his blood, how much more shall we be saved
from God's wrath through him! For if, when
we were God's enemies, we were reconciled to
him through the death of his Son, how much
more, having been reconciled, shall we be

saved through his life! Not only is this so, but we also rejoice in God through our Lord Jesus Christ, through whom we have now received reconciliation.

—ROMANS 5:1–11

chapter 3

THE GREATEST GAME: THE ESSENCE OF LOVE

AVID GOLFERS HAVE a love affair with the game. It is in their souls. Their days' activities are planned around their game, and if there are frost delays, it could mean that all of their daylight hours are given over to golf. Golfers must set up tee times* days in advance. As he steps up to the tee, a golfer's first thought is to make contact with the ball. (Remember, mine sometimes goes backwards.) The average able-bodied golfer will hit the ball, and it will take flight down the fairway. Hitting the ball long and straight is the goal.

---

* A tee time does not mean sharing a cup of tea before playing; it's when golfers and their playing partners are scheduled to start. Starting to play a round of golf means that a golfer will place a dimpled golf ball on a little wooden or plastic stick known as a tee, and then swing away.

Golfers have a wardrobe and equipment that belong solely to the game. Thankfully, Bob has never been much for pastels, Bermuda shorts, or argyle. Many will pay hundreds of dollars for the right club or the latest putter. Also, professional male golfers use a white ball, as does Bob; they refuse to use a pink, orange, or yellow ball.* Many golfers pay hundreds of dollars to play on the finest courses in the world. Unbelievably, a round of golf on some resort courses can cost $250 or more. Bob and others like him have made a substantial monetary investment in this sport over the years, but it is and continues to be a great love affair for them. Lord knows, if He comes to take Bob to his eternal home before me, I will undoubtedly be able to start my own pro shop with all the golf equipment stored in our garage.

A golfer's love for the game continues to play out whenever he or she strides to the first tee. You can spot a glint of hope that perhaps this round will

---

* I believe that it's perfectly fine for women to use different-colored golf balls. I know of one female professional who does, so it must be an accepted practice.

reveal a birdie or two and maybe, just maybe even an eagle.*

In the previous chapters, I've discussed two key ingredients to a happy marriage: the joy of listening and the importance of respect. Here I will share the third, and perhaps greatest, key—love. To better illustrate the blessing of our love, I want to tell you about Bob's parents, his daughter Teri, my family, Bob's "sacrificial" love, and lastly, and most importantly, God's true sacrificial love.

Before Mary; his daughter Teri; and I came into Bob's life, his parents—Bob and Alice Snelling—were his greatest fans. They, too, had a love affair with the game of golf and helped Bob begin his journey with the game when he was twelve. Alice, during her early married years, worked as a personnel secretary in a school district. She also helped run a small business that belonged to her

---

* The terms *birdie* and *eagle* refer to the fewest strokes it takes to get the golf ball into the hole. An eagle means it took the golfer only two strokes under par to get the ball into the hole (i.e., if the hole was a par five, an eagle would be scored as a three). A birdie means it took the golfer one stroke under par to get the ball into the hole (i.e., using the same par-five example, a birdie would be scored as a four).

and Bob's dad. Bob's dad, in addition to running this business, was also the superintendent of mails and, for a time, postmaster for the Richmond, California, post office.

Bob was his parents' only son. Alice was a down-to-earth soul who was honest in her approach to life. She went to countless golf tournaments with her son, and she even served as his caddy.* Before you get upset, thinking, "Gee whiz, he let his mom pack around his clubs?" you must understand that doing this brought her great joy. I know. I talked with her any number of times about it, she was never happier than when she would relive those days with me. They were quite a pair. Bob and his mom could talk golf for hours on end.

I think, however, as much as Bob enjoyed this time with his mom, one of the proudest moments of his life was when he and his father won the California State father and son golf tournament.

As I've alluded to previously, at eighteen, Bob became a member of the Stanford University golf team. He was a very good golfer, though you will *never* hear him brag about past achievements.

---

* A caddy is someone who carries a golfer's clubs for him or her.

About the only thing he does do on occasion is to reminisce about past rounds, recalling fun or memorable holes or shots.

To me, he seems to remember every shot on every hole he has ever played. He claims I'm mistaken, but if I ask him, for example, What was your club selection two days ago on the seventeenth hole? I know that he would not only recall the specific club he used, but also how far the ball traveled when he hit it. I find this nothing short of amazing. I can't even remember what I had for lunch yesterday, let alone tell you what my club selection might have been on a particular hole. Even if you were to compare his love of golf to my love of shopping, I can't tell you what piece of clothing I bought most recently.

The days Bob spent with his parents enjoying the game are clearly among his most precious memories. His parents were very proud of him. Neither had any formal education, so they considered it very special that their son got into Stanford and had the privilege of playing on the golf team. While on the team, Bob was a scratch golfer, meaning that he consistently shot par or better. Back in those days, the professional golf tour did not pay the kind of handsome rewards that we hear about today. So, as

Bob was finishing up at Stanford in 1959, his only career choice was one that could guarantee him a steady income to support himself, his wife, and young daughter. However, if you ask him if he has any regrets about not turning professional, he says, "No way. My time with Mary and Teri was very important to me. Also, I never would have had the great opportunity that I had at the bank. The employees made my career incredible."

In his third year on the Stanford golf team, a tragedy befell Bob and his teammates. They were traveling by car on Highway 80 to Reno, Nevada, for a tournament. On a stretch of the highway that had only two lanes, a drunk driver in the oncoming lane crossed over the line, causing a head-on collision. The drunk driver was killed instantly. The driver of the car Bob was driving in did not die on the scene, but died from complications a few years after the accident.

Bob always remembers that awful afternoon and how, just after the accident, the driver of the car in which the team had traveled kept asking Bob to straighten out his leg. Bob told him that he was trying to, knowing that the driver's leg was severed and could not be straightened.

The two passengers in the back seat were treated at the hospital and released. Bob suffered a broken jaw, kneecap, and wrist. For several weeks, he had to take all of his meals through a straw, as his jaws had been wired shut to speed the healing. Unfortunately, when the emergency room doctors wired his jaw shut, they didn't do the job properly. Several weeks later, his jaw had to be broken again and reset. Additionally, the impact from that collision has caused Bob years of skeletal pain as well as degenerative arthritis in his spine.

Ever since the accident, Bob has lived in constant pain. He cannot sleep at night, as it is just too uncomfortable in his spine and neck. He has tried many kinds of beds and pillows to get some relief. He has had numerous MRIs, and the doctors have told him that his back and neck were severely traumatized.

As incredible as this may seem, Bob believes his pain is a reminder that he could have lost his life that day but instead, God spared him. That is how my incredible husband approaches this tragedy. There are days when I can see the pain on his face, yet he smiles and goes about his business. He never lets on to friends or family how much he suffers on a daily basis. However, I think his parents must have seen on his face what I see every day, for parents seem to know everything.

Bob's dad passed away in 2002. (I've noted that his name was also Bob; however, my Bob is not a "junior," as they have different middle names.) My father-in-law died at age ninety-one from pneumonia. He was very handy at fixing things around the house. I can't imagine how that gene didn't pass to his son. He was very bright and had a keen sense about people. My Bob did get both those genes. Bob's dad was a great local history buff and could recount the smallest of details. The latter we know was passed on to my Bob, as you will recall his ability to tell a story and to remember the particular clubs he uses on each hole of golf.

Alice, Bob's mom, died in 2003, a few days after we had celebrated her ninety-first birthday. She was quite lucid even on the day before she passed. Bob and I will never forget the night before she passed away. While she slept in a hospital bed in our bedroom, she uttered "Happy, happy, happy" over and over. The next day, I asked her why she kept repeating those words. She replied, "I just want happiness for you two always." She got her last wish.

Bob's parents were hard-working, self-reliant individuals who I was proud to know for a brief time. The love the three of them shared was something to behold. I've given you some insight into who Bob's parents were, as I think it explains a lot about him. They instilled in him the values of independence and self-reliance. They also allowed him to just be. Naturally, they disciplined him when necessary, but they were supportive of all his decisions, including his dedication to the game of golf, the fact that he and Mary chose to elope, and his decision to bring me into his life.

I was in my early thirties when I first met Bob's parents. Bob was fifty-seven, and they were in their early eighties. They were never judgmental. They said, "If she makes you happy, then that is all that matters to us."

Because my father had passed away when I was twenty, Bob's dad agreed to give me away when Bob and I were married in Kona, Hawaii. This was the first time in their lives that Bob's parents had been on an airplane. I will never forget Bob's dad asking me, as we were just about to be transported to the lagoon where his son and I were to be married, "Why are you so nervous?" I started to cry as I replied, "I just want to make Bob happy." He said, "Don't worry; he is and you will."

Bob's parents gave him a start in life that many children envy. It was a privilege for me to be able to glimpse this happy trio. I couldn't believe how purely and sweetly they all seemed to live for each other. Their love was a perfect blessing from God. This love carries over to Bob and Mary's only daughter, Teri. She is married to a wonderful man named Terry. (Bob's parents started calling him "Terrance" to cut down on the confusion.) Together, Teri and Terry have two energetic, athletic, and happy boys named Cameron and Austin. Teri has a beautiful, loving, and caring daughter named Stacy from a previous marriage. Bob has told me that Teri's relationship with her mother was among the dearest of mother-daughter relationships.

I met Teri for the first time a couple of years after Mary died. I was very nervous, not to mention afraid of that first meeting. While Bob was recovering from surgery, I went to his house to take him some lasagna. I rang the doorbell, and Teri answered. Seeing me was quite a shock for her, because I am also a few years younger than she. Bob had mentioned me before to her, but I don't think she realized until that moment just how serious this relationship had become. I know it was hard for her, yet she handled our meeting with grace and love.

What a privilege it is for me to have Teri and her family in my life. Clearly, she and her children are a marvelous extension of Bob. I can see him in each of them.

Cameron, the oldest, who is now sixteen, has a calm and caring persona. He focuses completely on what other people are saying. He loves all sports, especially basketball, and music, just like his Papa —his grandfather, Bob.

Austin has a happy-go-lucky spirit and a quick wit. He loves baseball and playing computer games. He keeps us all laughing when we get together. He is quite the charmer—again, just like his Papa.

Stacy is kind, gentle, and patient, with a nurturing spirit, which is why she makes the perfect nurse. Her thoughtfulness and love for her family must be quite similar to her Grandmother Mary's character. I also see much of Bob in her.

I can't possibly replace the love that only a

grandmother would have given them. I feel terrible for what it must mean for Teri and her kids to not have Mary here. I am so sorry that she cannot attend the basketball and baseball games, see pictures of the proms or the first dances, and enjoy holiday get-togethers. How proud she would have been to see Stacy walk across the stage when she graduated from nursing school, though I'm sure her spirit must have been there. When we come together as a family, I see Bob in all of them, and it fills me with an indescribable joy. Teri and I grow closer each year, and I am so thankful for her friendship and love. She, too, knows that for me, her father's happiness is paramount.

My parents, Ted and Betty Poage, were two of the most generous people I will ever know. I was a selfish child, and so I posthumously apologize to them and of course to my sister, Jackie, thankfully still with me today, for having to endure my selfish ways. Jackie and I are growing closer each year. I am confident that it was my selfishness that kept us from growing closer sooner. She has been married to my brother-in-law, Merrill, for thirty years and has three beautiful children, each with unique talents and gifts. I can see my parents in each of them, as well.

Jennifer is my oldest niece. She has a loving, generous spirit and does her best to take care of those in need around her. Brian, my only nephew, has a very quick wit and is exceptionally bright. My youngest niece, Chelsea, is my "love bug." She has a very keen sense of people and shows remarkable patience, for one so young, with those around her in need.

Once again, it is a blessing beyond belief to have these six children—Stacy, Cameron, Austin, Jennifer, Brian, and Chelsea—in my life. They are God's gifts to me. I love them with all that I am. Thanks, too, to my wonderful sister for putting up with me for all of these years.

My dad, a veteran of the Second World War,* was a waist gunner in the Air Force who flew on B-17s. His plane was shot down on July 8, 1944, over France, and he was imprisoned for ten months. He was first held in Stalag Luft IV in Poland, but he also endured the Hanover March, in which he and

---

* I would like to credit my sister, who is very good with details, for filling in the blanks in the following account of our dad's war experience.

the other prisoners marched for eighty days during Europe's coldest winter in more than one hundred years. Thousands of marchers died. He was then held in Stalag Luft 11B until he and others were liberated on April 16, 1945. I don't think any of us can imagine what a terrible ordeal this must have been for him, as well as the many others who suffered with him. We Americans must always remember to give thanks to our veterans who fought in this war and the many who died so that we can be free. Thank you, vets. You are loved and greatly appreciated!

Some of my fondest childhood memories were of my dad taking me to Oakland Athletics' baseball games. This probably explains my passion for the game. What a great dad I had! I regret that I didn't tell him that more often.

My mother passed away in 2006. If I told you her age, undoubtedly her spirit would haunt me, as she held her age close to her vest. My mom was very generous with my sister and me. She volunteered at the local hospital for many years after my father passed. During the Second World War, she drove a Red Cross ambulance that delivered blood supplies to the ships at the ports in Oakland, California.

She rarely spent any money on herself. After my father passed away, my sister and I would encourage her to take a cruise or do some traveling, but that was not of interest to her. She lived out her final days in a care home near my sister. I repeatedly asked her to live with us here in Arizona, but she said, "I wouldn't live near a cactus." I know she wanted to be near her grandchildren. During the last years of her life, I was able to see her once a month, and we talked every day on the phone. The pain of her death is a hard one, especially around the holidays, as I think she enjoyed opening up packages as much as any child does. One of the first things I will do in heaven, if given the opportunity, is to thank both my parents for their selflessness, love, and generosity toward me.

I hope I have not bored you with my "family videotape," but I believe that the love that Bob and I share, and the freedom we have to enjoy our love is perhaps best understood by outlining our support system. Our greatest downfall in returning the love to our support system has been the fact that we did not do enough to speak the Word of God to our parents.

When my dad passed, I was self-involved and

didn't know Christ. As for my mom, she knew how important Christ had become in my life. Each time I would visit, she would tell me, "Next time you visit, let's go to church." Well, when the next time to visit rolled around, she would be either too tired or not feeling well, so it never happened. I don't fault her for that; it was understandable. At her age, she could certainly have felt badly from one day to the next. Although she suffered from dementia in her last days, it was a fall in 2006 that ultimately led to her death. Because my sister contacted a Presbyterian minister just days before my mom died, we are now confident of my mom's salvation.

In my mom's last days, while she was under hospice care and sedated to keep her comfortable, I read to her from the Books of Galatians and Colossians. We were told by the folks at hospice that hearing is the last sense to leave a person, so it was important for me to know that God's words were among the last she would hear.

As for Bob's parents and their salvation, we are less certain. My words to Bob's mom as I would tell her of that Sunday's sermon or try to tell her the story of Jesus' birth, seemed to be jumbled and lacking in clarity. I am not sure if she ever really knew Christ. I read Psalm 23 at her bedside when she passed, but I failed her and our Lord here; God forgive me.

As for Bob's dad, when Bob asked for the hospital chaplain to baptize him, Bob's dad was in a coma. He could not speak the words that he accepted Christ as his Lord and Savior. We both live with this regret each day, as we now understand that evangelizing is the Great Commission. Pastor McFarland has been a great comfort here, telling us, "We never know a person's heart in their final moments. It is possible they come to Christ on their own at the last. Christ gives each of us every possible opportunity."

What was wrong with me, though, that I couldn't speak the words that would help them know our Savior? Shame on me for not ensuring their salvation earlier! Our parents were given to us by God to love us, protect us, and to nurture us. Just as in the game of golf, our parents helped tee up our younger days. In Bob's case, they made sure that he met his tee time; in my case, my folks made sure that I was at my Bluebird and Job's Daughter's meetings on time.

Just as golfers wear appropriate attire, our parents

gave us clothing to fit any occasion. Like the golfers who pay handsomely to play, our parents paid hundreds of thousands of dollars for our care. They gave us the necessary accoutrement we needed to live our lives in love. All four of our parents played a perfect round as earthly parents, and our hearts are forever grateful to them—and of course to God for giving them to us!

Now I have to tell you what a toll Bob's love for me has taken on three aspects of his body: his shoulders, his knees, and his sleep patterns.

Bob's shoulders have not only been offered up as pillows on plane flights, but also have carried the weight of any issue we have had. I have cried on his shoulders time and again. You may not imagine that there have been any tearful moments in our marriage, but there have been. There have been frustrations with work or school, frustrations with certain family situations, and frustrations with health issues for friends, family members, or for Bob. All of these frustrations amount to that little thing we refer to as life.

Like me, when your husband or wife is hurting or undergoes surgery and then rehabilitation, all you want to do is to take his or her place and stop the suffering. Can you imagine how God has done this for every one of us?

During our relationship, Bob and I have each had four surgeries. He has had prostate and bladder surgeries. He has also had both knees replaced *at the same time.* In all cases, he was the best patient that the doctors, nurses, and I have ever been around. About an hour after his knee-replacement surgery, the nurses stood him up next to the bed. He let out one scream that could be heard around the hospital. After that, he never complained. I spent the nights with him in a recliner next to his hospital bed in case he needed something during the night, as I knew he hated to bother the nurses. I give all praise and glory to God for healing him and sending him the best surgeon and physical therapists. It has been five years since his surgery, and again praise to the divine Healer that Bob's new knees are doing great!

However, before his surgery, Bob was in excruciating pain. Not only did that car accident leave him with one bad knee, he inherited bad knees from his father. For many years, both of his knees were just bone grinding against bone. Again though, even during that pain, Bob never complained. I could, however, see the pain on his face with each step. Why did he wait so long to have surgery? He was waiting for a few things.

First, he wanted the procedure to improve to the point that he wouldn't need to have a second surgery in a few years. (As it was, this surgery took five hours and of course many weeks of rehabilitation.) Second, he was waiting to find the right surgeon. Lastly, and this is where the sacrificial love for me comes in, he did not want me to have to take care of his mother alone if something negative happened to him during the surgery.

I have already mentioned that, after Bob's dad passed away in 2002, we brought his mother, Alice, home to Arizona to live with us. Although she was in great health for a ninety year old, she had an untreatable type of macular degeneration, a condition of the eyes that takes away one's sight. Because she was very independent, she suffered mightily without sufficient sight.

Caring for someone who wants to care for herself but cannot is daunting at times. Admittedly, I did not, in many moments, show her the grace that she deserved. Even though I didn't start out feeling this way, I grew to feel bitter toward her and even toward God. Bob realized this, and even though he never said anything at the time, I knew that a large reason for his putting his surgery on hold was to help me. I pray he can forgive me for my selfishness. I believe now that God has forgiven me. I just wish I could forgive myself, for in this instance I am certain I never will.

My selfishness kept me from being the best helpmate for my selfless husband. I'll give you another example of my selfishness, as if you needed one. When we first brought Alice to Arizona, our house was not laid out in such a way that three people could live in it comfortably. So, Bob had a bigger home built for the three of us: half of it for Alice, and half of it for us. Unfortunately, Alice died two weeks before we moved into the new house. Now we have a big home that, in this current housing market, we couldn't begin to sell for even close to what we paid to build it.

Alice passed away in November 2003, and Bob finally had his knee surgery in June 2004. He had an incredible surgeon and excellent physical therapists. I tried to redeem myself by attempting to be the kind of nurse he needed. He never suggested that I needed to redeem myself for anything, but he knew that having his mother with us had been stressful for me. He never said anything to me about my selfishness, but I knew how I was.

If you aren't disgusted with me by now for my selfishness, you should be. The last area where Bob has sacrificed his body for me is through his sleep. He and I are both "worry warts." I usually get short and/or cry when I worry. He, on the other hand, loses countless hours of sleep worrying about me. He worries about our finances, wondering whether or not there will be enough left for me if something happens to him first. He also wonders if leaving work was the right decision for me, and if I'm really happy.

I wish he wouldn't worry, because he brings me such indescribable and incomparable joy that there is nothing to fret about. In fact, one of the sweetest moments in my entire life was waking up in the hospital after a surgery in the wee morning hours and seeing Bob's face. He was there at my bedside, with a smile and a gleam in his eye, telling me that the surgery went fine. Being with him is the most comforting feeling I have ever known. Oh, how I love this man.

I have to share one last story of his sacrificial

giving that has a little laughter and a lot of irony. Several years ago, we went on a romantic Valentine's Day getaway to a mountain retreat in Big Sur, California. For whatever reason, there were so many flies buzzing around the back porch of our cabin that it was as if one of the plagues had been unleashed again. I had gone to the retreat's lobby area to get some refreshments. While Bob was alone in the cabin, trying to rid the porch of the flies so we could enjoy our refreshments outside, he found some fly paper. (Apparently, there was a supply of fly paper in one of the closets, as this was an ongoing problem.) In his quest to create a perfect mood, he decided to hang the flypaper. And what piece of equipment did he stand on to hang the paper? Why, a rocking chair, of course. Much like the screwdriver incident that I mentioned in the Introduction, what would make him believe that a rocking chair was the right tool? Needless to say, when he stood on the rocking chair, he fell.

Of course, when I returned to the cabin, he didn't tell me immediately that he had fallen. In fact, we were halfway through our refreshments when he told me that his side was hurting and explained what had happened. I wanted to take him to an emergency room, but he refused. After we returned home, I insisted that he see his doctor, who determined that he had a broken rib. Isn't it ironic that Bob broke a rib while trying to help his helpmate, or "rib"? (His "rib," namely me, admittedly is broken in more ways than one.)

Not only am I a selfish sinner, broken and torn, but I can best characterize myself most times as a "mess." I already told you what a klutz I can be, but I am cynical, impatient, and, more often than not, lacking grace for others. And this is only the half of it! How is it that even in my brokenness, God can possibly forgive me? That is why I must tell this story. Thanks to God for giving me a second chance at so many things. Although I didn't have a second chance with Bob's mom, I think that I did the best job I knew with my own mom in the last years of her life. Only God can judge, and He most certainly will as I stand before Him on that day. This second chance that God has given me has certainly come at a hefty price, though. It comes by God's saving and sacrificial love of His Son, Jesus Christ.

So, yes, it is true, I adore Bob for his sacrificial giving, but it is Christ whom I worship. I know in my heart that were it not for Christ sending Bob into my life, I would never have been able to return God's love. I think it is interesting that the first time love is mentioned in the Bible is in Genesis 22:2, "Then God said, 'Take your son, your only son, Isaac, whom you love, and go to the region of Moriah. Sacrifice him there as a burnt offering on one of the mountains I will tell you about.'" We know that God ultimately did not make Abraham sacrifice Isaac, but God then knew how much Abraham loved him by willingly going to the mountain with his son. God, however, did sacrifice His only Son for us, a sacrifice that none of us can possibly imagine!

I often think about how God first loved me and that sacrifice, how He knew me before I was born, how He spoke me into my mother's womb, how He knew I would fall in love with Bob. He knew what a selfish child and adult I would be. He knew about all the times I made mistakes, and yet He forgave me. He loves me.

I would like to share an acronym that I came up with for the word *love* that brings everything

together for me about how I feel for our Lord and
His love. I hope it will be a way to help remind you
of that same love that He also has for you.

   L — Lord,
   O — Our
   V — Very
   E — Essence

This acronym helps me know that He is with
me and in me and wants the best for me. He is my
essence, though I reject Him time and time again.
Sending Bob to me was the greatest gesture of His
love that I can imagine. That's why I wrote this
book.

Thanks to God for sending me loving parents
and a wonderful sister and brother-in-law with
three beautiful children. To Him is the glory for
allowing awesome in-laws, a fun-loving and caring
stepdaughter and son-in-law, and their amazing
children to brighten my life. Thanks also for all of
the incredible friends who fill our days with such
happy and cherished moments. How blessed we
are to have known the love of all these dear, dear
people.

So, what can best be said then about my love

affair with Bob? My feelings are summarized by a quotation by Sarah Pinkerton, the wife of one of our founding fathers, who said, "I have as great an affinity for him as ever existed between two mortals." That captures it completely for me! Bob is my everything, and he is from my essence, my Lord and Savior, Christ Jesus.

Perhaps most important is for me to share with you how greatly blessed I feel to know God's love. I pray that you feel His essence each day of your life, too. He shows us in so many ways. He sends us friends, family, incredible spouses, and yes, even the game of golf to show us how much he cares.

Chapter Activity

Do you scrapbook? It seems as if many of my friends are gifted in this way. If you are into scrapbooking, you can concentrate on our Lord's love or His essence in your life and create a scrapbook about that love. Can you imagine how that kind of project could be handed down from generation to generation? It would be amazing. Each of us has a story to share about His essence. We have pictures of our precious spouses, our children, grandchildren, and extended family. Pictures say a thousand words, so why not put them all into one scrapbook that would show your family how God is at work in your life? Now, maybe you are like me and are not very creative. How about making the scrapbook a family project? You could buy all the necessary materials, invite your family to come over for dinner, and, as a family, you could show God's love at work in your family's life.

If scrapbooking doesn't appeal to you, how about making a weekly date with your spouse? You could have a standing date, say on Friday nights, and take time to be together. On our date night, Bob and I usually wear attire that is a bit fancier than just jeans. Bob breaks out dress slacks for this occasion. I try to wear something that I know will please him. This weekly activity goes a very long way to share your love, God's essence, with each other.

Prayer Time

Now, here is my final prayer question for you: How do I show love for what God has done for me in my life? Do I love my spouse as I promised I would in God's sight on the day that I said, "I will"? Do I love him or her each and every day in each and every way? Do I show my spouse the same love that God has shown me?

If you answered yes to all of the questions above, please offer thanks to God for sending you the capacity to love. If you answered no to any of these questions, can you pinpoint the "why" behind your no answer? Do you think that maybe you suffer from the same malady that I do, the one called selfishness? Are you taking all your blessings for granted and needing to be reminded of those blessings each day? Take heart. Careful examination and an honest appraisal of your shortcomings is a good thing. It is a step in God's direction.

So, now that you know this, take that next step. Find the best way—your way—to tell or show your spouse how much and why you love him or her. Be sure, too, to thank your spouse for his or her love, and thank God for His love, too.

> *Dear God, thank You so much for sending me an amazing, selfless, and wonderful husband to love. You have blessed me in countless ways, dear God. Forgive me when my selfish ways interfere with my recognition of Your essence in my life. I am truly nothing without You and Your saving grace and mercy. You are my Lord;*

*You are my essence. I love and worship
You now and always. Amen.*

If I speak in the tongues of men and of angels,
but have not love, I am only a resounding
gong or a clanging cymbal. If I have the gift
of prophecy and can fathom all mysteries
and all knowledge, and if I have a faith that
can move mountains, but have not love, I am
nothing. If I give all I possess to the poor and
surrender my body to the flames, but have
not love, I gain nothing. Love is patient, love
is kind. It does not envy, it does not boast,
it is not proud. It is not rude, it is not self-
seeking. It is not easily angered; it keeps no
record of wrongs. Love does not delight in evil
but rejoices with the truth. It always protects,
always trusts, always hopes, always perseveres.
Love never fails. But, where there are proph-
esies, they will cease; where there are tongues,
they will be stilled; where there is knowledge,
it will pass away. For we know in part and we
prophesy in part, but when perfection comes,
the imperfect disappears. When I was a child,
I talked like a child, I thought like a child. I
reasoned like a child. When I became a man, I
put childish ways behind me. Now we see but
a poor reflection as in a mirror; then we shall

see face to face. Now I know in part; then I shall know fully, even as I am fully known. And now these three remain: faith, hope, and love. But the greatest of these is love.

—1 CORINTHIANS 13

My lover spoke and said to me, "Arise, my darling, my beautiful one, and come with me. See! The winter is past; the rains are over and gone."

—SONG OF SONGS 2:10–11

For God so loved the world that He gave His one and only Son, that whoever believes in Him shall not perish but have eternal life. For God did not send His Son into the world to condemn the world, but to save the world through Him.

—JOHN 3:16–17

Let love and faithfulness never leave you; bind them around your neck, write them on the tablet of your heart.

—PROVERBS 3:3

Through love and faithfulness sin is atoned for; through the fear of the LORD a man avoids evil.

—PROVERBS 16:6

Love and faithfulness keep a king safe, through love his throne is made secure.

—PROVERBS 20:28

He who pursues righteousness and love finds life, prosperity and honor.

—PROVERBS 21:21

CONCLUSION: THE NINETEENTH HOLE

I N THE INTRODUCTION, I mentioned that the nineteenth hole is an opportunity for a golfer to hopefully unwind and attempt to regain some joy from what can sometimes be a harrowing event. As I come to the end of this book, I find that I have experienced great joy in being able to express myself to you. This book has been about sharing with you my gratitude to Him for sending me unconditional love. To me, His role in that is undeniable. I hope you have felt my heart as I have shared my gratefulness. I am so happy I have had the opportunity to share with you how blessed I feel with God's grace and the second chance he has offered me for a perfect love. Praise God, He is indeed a perfect God. Thank you for indulging me and being such a patient audience.

I find myself now in a position of needing to explain to you that the memories of a promiscuous youth, recreational drug use, and a failed first marriage are not even blips on the scale of harrowing events for me in my life. I now glimpse my mortality, and I am still most grateful to Him.

Several months ago, in a routine exam, one of my blood tests revealed a very low white blood cell count. After further testing, it has been determined that I may indeed be in the early stages of leukemia. Apparently, my doctor has followed these levels for a while now, and they have been decreasing each year. The only way to know for certain if I have leukemia is to undergo a bone marrow study. I have heard this procedure is quite painful, so for now I intend to hold off on having it done. It's odd in today's medical world, with its great advances, that this study is the only answer. Apparently, if I were to have the procedure, and if the results were to come back positive, nothing could be done to prevent the progression of the disease.

I monitor my white blood cell count every few months, and for now I feel great. I am not sharing my medical news with you so that you will feel bad for me; I may simply be one of those rare folks with a low white blood cell count. I have seen many people—some within my church family, both in California and here in Arizona—who are much younger than I and who suffer mightily with a variety of diseases. However, they endure their suffering courageously and with little fanfare. So, please do not misunderstand; I am not asking for your pity. However, if the Lord is soon to call me home, I don't want to have missed out on sharing with you and with anyone willing to listen, how much Bob's love has meant to me. Especially, and more importantly, I wanted you to know how thankful I am to my Lord, my essence, for allowing me a second chance for a "perfect" love, no matter how long He allows it to last in this world. I don't know the best way to end this story or the best way to share with you the importance of valuing your life mate. I have tried to share with you the importance of humor, listening, respect, and love as it relates to marriage. Perhaps you have your own special ingredients to a successful marriage. I would love to hear your story.

My prayer for each of you is that you will have the opportunity to live each day of your life, and of course your marriage, on the first tee. You may not, in a literal sense, ever have such an opportunity, and maybe you really wouldn't want to live on a golf course. But, remember, from a figurative sense, living your marriage on the first tee means that you, too, can experience your kind of perfect with your spouse. But are you both willing to let God into your lives? Until that happens, you may not truly recognize your blessing.

Living on the first tee means that you can experience great hope. The hope that a golfer experiences when he steps into that first tee box means that he just might best his previous score during the day's outing. Maybe, like me, if this is your second marriage, or even if you are blissfully happy in your first marriage, then you know that each new day with your spouse offers you the hope of understanding what it means to be happy in your marriage. In my humble opinion, this kind of happiness only comes from God.

Living on the first tee in your marriage means that you can, at every turn, learn to appreciate the joy that God has given us as husband and wife. Golfers experience similar joy when they connect with the ball off of the tee and it ends up hundreds of yards down the fairway. If you don't feel joy in your marriage, ask yourself why. You don't want your days to pass you both by without it.

Ladies and gentlemen, have a reality check with each other. Chances are, if you are not feeling a sense of joy, your spouse may not be either. This can be tricky because, as we know, your spouse may see life a little differently at times than you do. Let's face it; men and women communicate differently. You may recall that when I was completing work on my master's degree, I had to prepare thirteen drafts of my thesis. My topic was gender differences in leadership style. My findings were probably of no surprise to you; I discovered that a man will prefer a more autocratic leadership style and a woman will prefer a more democratic style. Granted, this study was with men and women who were in leadership roles, as opposed to husband and wife, but it still speaks to different communication styles. My findings led me to believe that men are more comfortable when they can be task-oriented in their approach to leadership. Women, on the other hand, want to approach leadership in a more harmonious fashion. We women want to involve people in decisions, rather than just telling them what needs to be done. (However, there is an exception to this, and that is when women are leading other women. The tendency in that case is for women leaders to adopt a more autocratic or task-oriented approach.)

The point here is that men and women communicate differently. Again, this is not news to anyone. I share it with you only insofar as you may need to seek help in talking to your spouse when and if it comes to telling him or her that you lack joy in your marriage. Each needs to know but must hear it in a gentle way. If you don't feel as if you can express yourself in a way that will best be received, then perhaps you should seek professional counseling before you approach your spouse. Also, be sure to carefully examine your prayer life. God does listen, but if you aren't talking to Him with any regularity and only on your terms He may not deliver the answer in your timeframe.

Finally, living on the first tee means freedom. This could be easily misconstrued as a lack of accountability to your spouse. What I refer to here is learning to let your spouse be. We don't have to change one thing about him or her. We can just let him or her be who God intended *and* be happy with that—can't we? I pray that God brings you and your spouse the opportunity to recognize hope, joy, and freedom in your marriage. He has given me that second chance. He will give that to you, too, if you let Him.

Thank you again for letting me share my testimony and to pour out my heart. Thanks to all of you serious golfers for letting a hack into your life. If there are any hacks out there not taking their marriage or their golf game seriously, my prayer is that they will start each day, or the next time they are on the first tee, saying to God, "OK, I'm ready to grip it and rip it." This means praying, "I am ready to give it my all, God. I know I may have not done so well in previous rounds, but with you as my caddy, carrying my life's bags, I have the best shot for a second chance of living every day on the first tee."

> Trust in the LORD with all your heart and lean not on your own understanding. In all your ways acknowledge Him and he will make your paths straight.
>
> —PROVERBS 3:5–6

AFTERWORD

THE SONG "ONCE AGAIN" by Matt Redman perfectly depicts my gratitude to God. To listen to it, go to my Web site, www.heartofthecrossbooks.com.

ABOUT THE AUTHOR

CAROLYN SNELLING AND her husband, Bob, live in Surprise, Arizona. She holds a master's of science degree in psychology and is currently working toward her doctorate in organizational leadership. For seventeen years she worked in the secular world in both the human resources and public relations fields. For the last few years she has worked and volunteered in the Radiant Church ministry.

TO CONTACT THE AUTHOR

WWW.HEARTOFTHECROSSBOOKS.COM

The following is an excerpt from the Introduction to Carolyn Snelling's soon-to-come novel, *Eagle:*

ALTHOUGH I WROTE *Mulligan* to honor God and marriage, it also revealed my unenviable status as a golfing hack. I don't really care about the game, though I will watch a portion of a major tournament on television, but that's only to spend time with my wonderful hubby. Thank God for TiVo and DVRs. Stick me with a needle, poke a stick in my eye, but please, please don't ask me to spend four hours playing the game.

So, if indeed the game is so unimportant to me, why on Earth am I so bothered by the adage "not feeling up to par"? I can't get my brain around how that phrase wants to draw a correlation to "par" in golf. Yes, I understand the adage refers to *par* as something normal. But what the underlying meaning misses badly is that serious golfers always hope their score will be well *under* par.

After fourteen years of marriage to such a person, I have come to understand that par is not all that great.

As a Christian, does it intrigue you as it does me to pursue the idea that maybe we should live our lives under par? Following God in all His ways shouldn't mean treating life as normal or business as usual. The choice we have freely made to accept Him in our hearts, our minds, and our souls should give us pause each day to rethink how we embrace our lives. Shouldn't it?

In golf, some under-par terms are *birdie* and *eagle*. If par on a particular golf hole is five, a birdie on that same hole means it only took four shots for the ball to make its way into the cup, and an eagle refers to three shots. An eagle, then, is considered two shots under par.

As an eagle will change a round of golf, how would living each day "two shots under par" change our lives as Christians? I can't tell you the times I get caught up in my daily activities and conveniently choose to forget my Christianity.

I get impatient with the clerk at the grocery store for not checking me out of line fast enough. Yet, do

I stop to think how she may not be going home to a husband as loving as mine?

I get angered when a boss gives me grief over a report that missed the mark. Yet, do I stop to realize that he may have done me a favor by improving my future reports?

I get fearful of flying in airplanes. Yet, do I stop to realize that I am a child of God and His will be done?

No, often I do not live my life under par, let alone two under par. I do not soar like an eagle, either. Eagles are creatures that seem to exude a sense of grace. Furthermore, they have been listed on the endangered species list. As a Christian, I should recognize that my walk is indeed something to be handled in a precious manner. I should take on a flight pattern that exudes grace and a recognition that My God thinks of me as His rare and precious child. He cares for me like no other. He cares for you in that way, too. I should treat you that way, also.

This book will explore eagles that I have witnessed and how they soar for God and what we can learn from them. We can and should stretch our reach on His behalf in every interaction. I want to be an eagle. I want to be under par for God. Join me as we go for the green in two and take flight for God!